Once Upon a Midnight Scroll

Poems for the Overstimulated & Disillusioned

Heidi Becker

Andrews McMeel
PUBLISHING®

for open ears, wandering minds,
and lost hearts that ache for the hope
of a happy-ish fairy-tale ending

The authorised representative in the EEA is Simon and Schuster
Netherlands BV, Herculesplein 96 3584 AA Utrecht, Netherlands.
(info@simonandschuster.nl)

Andrews McMeel Publishing
a division of Andrews McMeel Universal
1130 Walnut Street, Kansas City, Missouri 64106

www.andrewsmcmeel.com

Cover art: *Lady Lilith*, watercolor and gouache, The Metropolitan
Museum of Art, Dante Gabriel Rossetti (British, 1828–1882)
and Henry Treffry Dunn (British, 1838–1899)

26 27 28 29 30 SHD 10 9 8 7 6 5 4 3 2 1

ISBN: 979-8-8816-0821-7

Library of Congress Control Number: 2026931384

FSC
www.fsc.org
MIX
Paper | Supporting
responsible forestry
FSC® C008955

Contents

Alice Down the Pixelated Rabbit Hole

I've been popping bottled-up thoughts
Sipping on sparkling pink prosecco
Three screens, a journal, and a pen
But I think it's less the bubbles
And more the pixels
That are going to my head

Drunk on a doomscroll, my inhibitions lowered
The self-doubt creeps through the insecure cracks
That cause a chasm called the digital abyss
I follow the blue light and fall like Alice
Down the rabbit hole of a drunken doomscroll

Lost in the labyrinth of who I am and who I want to be
Trying to decide which fig I should pick off of Sylvia Plath's tree
When doubt clouds roll in
And I don't think I possess the talent to deserve the juiciest fig

The disorienting labyrinth leads me to a reflective pool
Mirror, Mirror
I think it's cursed because it only shows my flaws
The water invites me to jump in
To wash away all that's wrong

Sinking further into the Land of Make-Believe
I purchase a personality and products to make me pretty
I follow a yellow brick road to meet the man behind the screen
Which turns out to be all algorithmic code
Manipulated by the evil kings on the throne

Will I get my happily ever after, ever?
All the pixelated princes turn to ghosts
As the Land of Make-Believe announces

The price of happiness is half off!

My doomscroll hangover starts to fizzle out
As the blue light that pulled me in fades to black
Blinking through a pixelated disenchantment
I leave my phone unplugged for a bit
And explore my bottled-up thoughts on a walk instead
Where the trees, the grass, the sky, and the leaves
Look just the same as when I was a kid
Maybe *everything* isn't *all* so bad
In the Land of Make-Believe

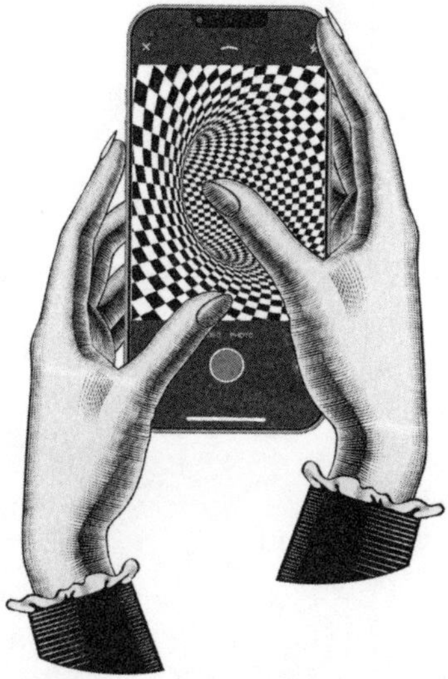

Lost in the Labyrinth

If You Don't Like This, I'm Sorry

I'm *SO* sorry
Don't look at my hair
It's so embarrassing
I haven't been to the salon in months
So I've been claiming that it's *old-money bronde*

I'm *SO* sorry
Don't look at my nails
They're broken, brittle, and frail

I'm *SO* sorry
Don't look at my face
I've been breaking out recently
Not the adult cystic acne

I'm *SO* sorry
About how I look
Or if I've overdressed
Or overstepped
Or called too much attention to myself
Or if you think I'm cringe
And don't get the satire
Of my online language

I'm *SO* sorry
That as a woman I've been conditioned
To feel *SO* sorry
And to consider how I appear
And how it might make *you* feel

I'm *SO* sorry
If you think that's overdramatic
Or incorrect

I'm *SO* sorry
If I didn't leave you the space to perceive me
Before I opened up with my own insecurity
As a way to demonstrate my self-awareness
Inadvertently having the opposite effect

I'm *SO* sorry
If I come across as insecure and in my head
And that if you compliment me
I'll say thank you in appreciation
But not without a side of self-deprecation

I don't know if I do that for you or for me
Showing my vulnerability to put you at ease
Or if it's a subconscious self-defense mechanism
Because I sense you may be disingenuous

I'm *SO* sorry
If you didn't like this
I'm just as sick of myself saying the same habitual sorry
I can't help it; I've been programmed to please

To avoid conflict with every word I breathe
I extend my most insincere apologies

A Mosaic of Broken Glass

I used to see the glass as half full
But it slipped from my hand and shattered
The sharp shards piercing me in the foot
A disillusionment of false hope

The fragments cut deep
And I became hard
I thought being tough would get respect
But then it was said I was cold or callous
A *bitch*
Too stern? Too straightforward? Too vulgar?
I don't give a shit

But that's a bitchy lie
I do care
At least a little bit
Or else I wouldn't be writing this

So I thought humor would be a better vice
Another thing I've tried
But every time I get *all* the guys to laugh
It's a slanderous joke
At either my or some other woman's expense
But maybe it's not them; it's me
And I'm not cut out for comedy

So the mess of the broken glass
Still sparkles with the chunks
Of my cheerful disposition
That first stabbed me in the foot

Prompting a naive label
That struck a nerve
With slivers that sank into the skin
And drew blood from the deep cut of anger
Until the clunky bandage and clumsy limp
Served a bitch better as the punch line of a bit

But the pieces of the mess must be swept
So I've started gluing them back together again
To make a mosaic of my reckonings
A patchwork of treasured lessons
A montage of mirrors that deflect all the junk
That was once the cause
Of a cascade of pain in my foot

Checkmate

Oh, you're sad?
Well, they say
To let your salty tears fall to rid yourself of toxins
It'll fix your gut health and reduce your cortisol
But be conservative with your expressions
Or you'll deepen your lines and wrinkles
Then you'll look old, worthless, and invisible

They say to be sad, but not *too* sad
And to cry, yet to depuff your teary eyes
To face the world with a feminine smile
To smack a sweet sticker over your face
So a stranger doesn't walk by and say
You should smile more; you'd be prettier that way!

It's smile *MORE*
Till it's smile *LESS*

The conflicting messages ping-pong across your head
As you dive back and forth to hit the ball over the net
Keeping up a frantic one-woman volley of tears, cheers,
and sweat
To earn respect and play your way to a higher bracket of success

But with each tier, there are new rules and a new game
The courts are better, the 'fits are nicer
But the tears and sweat remain the same

Aren't you tired of paddling the ball
And pedaling the ping-ponging of the world's requests?
Maybe ping-pong is a pawn to keep us women too busy
To put our queens up against the kings in a game of chess

For our unhindered minds would have more time to strategize
If released from the volley between
The right way to love
The right way to age
The right way to cry
And the right way to express pain
Because without this weight
The kings might fear the growing threat
Of our unrestricted voices echoing
Checkmate
When we were only asking for a fair game

Lucky Puppet

Welcome to the puppet show
The strings of my marionette are long and clear
Sometimes I don't even notice them there
I don't always see the stage as I perform
Drifting into my own dance and song

Until I feel a little tug
As the corners of my mouth start to turn up
A reminder from the puppeteer
To be graceful and smile
And that *he* is still there
Pulling the strings
Directing the show

I don't mind doing the dance
For me, it's not *all* that bad

The puppeteer seems to like me
There are only so many good roles
But I always get cast
And even though the audience can get crass
Throw things and tell me I suck

I'm one of the *lucky* marionettes

It would feel wrong to not acknowledge
My privilege that got me the easier role
In the Patriarchy's Puppet Show

Lucky Puppet Inception

I'm a lucky puppet
As my strings are tugged before an audience
Who follow the theater rules in their rigid chairs
Enforced by the invisible system of puppeteers

From my onstage point of view
I catch an illuminated glimpse
Into the audience of men who *also* have strings
It's harder to notice, but they're part of the play, too

Attached to threads that direct them to react
In an acceptable masculine manner
Without tears, without fear
As emotions bubble up
But at the force of the puppeteers' tugs
They sit straight and bottle it up

Until the repression turns into a toxic outburst
Or they hate the puppets like me that get to perform
Or some of them notice the puppeteers overhead
That intertwine all of our strings to make a mess

An entangled jumble of chaos
That only works to the benefit
Of a select few powerful puppeteers
As they hoard the shows' profits
And pull the strings of our fingers to point at each other
From the audience to the performers
From the stage to the chairs

Princess-Treatment Preachers

I've been served social media sermons
With glittering but empty words
On how to become a *high-value woman*

As new creators chant and preach how to be
In your divine feminine
Lovely, modest, demure, sweet
Poised, fit, quiet, soft-spoken
In order to receive the treasured princess treatment

The promises sparkle with more glamour than the life of a wife
And dangle those little-girl dreams of princess royalty in front
of vulnerable eyes
That begin to believe their value is determined by the prince,
the prize
Only *if* they play the part to serve him just right
As if we are all not born with value
And have to follow a script to be recognized as high

As if I'm not worthy of flowers and door-holding
And don't have the respect from the person I'm dating
If I am who I am
Without following the directions on how to perform
Being a *high-value woman*

Why should I fold myself up and bend into a princess shape
Flattening into an illustrated picture in a storybook
Just to convince someone else I'm worthy of being treated
that way?

The storybook's cover might be titled with words of worth
Femininity, value, empowerment
Reaching with its tempting themes to pull me in
To live inside a two-dimensional fairy-tale castle
Drawn on the fantasy-filled pages within

I know once I'm in too deep
I'll realize how small it is
As the narrow walls start closing in
Making myself smaller and smaller
Sacrificing my grandness just to fit
One day, again, wondering
What life would be like outside of it

The preachers of princess treatment
Fail to mention that the old fables of princesses
Are frequent tales of loneliness, isolation, and manipulation
They strip down to an elementary definition of what it is to
be feminine
And lead us away from the real women who lead
The *modern* princesses with duties that blend with the masculine

The *real* princesses, our women leaders
Put up a fight to break down walled kingdoms
For *all* women's freedoms
Even those of the princess-treatment preachers
Who are under the kings' spells
Asking other women to follow the spiral staircase, as well
Till we get to the top of the castle's highest tower
And lured into a room called *princess treatment*
With a bolted door that slams shut and seals behind us

If I'm locked into being something that I'm not
I don't believe it is *me* holding the value and power
Just because my prince gives me a pretty room and brings
me flowers

THAT Girl Is Gone Monologue

THAT girl
That's always the defining compliment, isn't it?
She's THAT girl

Being THAT girl means she is a
Hot
Brilliant
Successful woman
Who adores a rigid routine, boutique Pilates, expensive products,
    and designer fashion
Who is ahead of the trends
Drinks hot water with lemon *every* morning
Loves a night out but *never* gets sloppy
Always says the right thing
Never has a blemish on her skin
And makes a nightly forty-five-minute skin-care routine
    look effortless
With products arranged into neat, pretty rows in her grand
    marble bathroom
While also heading to sleep with enough time to read fifty pages
Of her nonfiction self-improvement book before an eight-hour
    snooze

THAT girl is, above all, *hot*
Hot and successful
THAT girl never misses a day
You can tell by her perfect, slender, toned body
THAT girl will post an aesthetic photo of a sweet treat
But she'll take one bite and throw it away
She doesn't give in to what she craves
She flashes her perfect, pearly-white smile at men
And without fail, she attracts them

THAT girl has witty one-liners
And appeal that *always* gets her what she wants
Never rejected or ghosted
THAT girl is far too perfect to let go of

We think THAT girl actually exists
So we click the links and buy the things
For a THAT-girl experience
But even the examples we see of THAT girl
Have another THAT girl that they chase
In this endless THAT-girl race
Watching and dreaming of being
THAT girl
A projection of emotionless perfection that doesn't live
Outside of a curated, mechanical image

THAT girl isn't a real woman but a misogynistic myth
So is being THAT girl even *our own* wish?

Lip Gloss Isn't a Hobby of Girlhood

Aspiring TradWIFE
Or maybe MobWIFE
And when it's rock star it's
GIRLFRIEND
And when it's boss
It's GIRLboss

The internet says
It's giving girlhood
In the name of reclaiming *girl*
A fun reclamation that I, too, first partook in
Until it felt less a reclamation
And more an infantilization
That missed its own point and hurtled into viral counterproduction
Landing us back into a sweet, girly identity reduction

But don't cancel me if I say lip gloss isn't a hobby
Or label me now as a *pick-me*
Yet another bad type of girl to be

Obsessive Girl, Awkward Woman

Internet trends love girls
And girlhood
Favoring the pretty, playful girls
That might be naive
But the girls are fun; the girls are free

As a girl who has aged into her late twenties
I've witnessed an awkward hesitancy toward shifting identity
Away from the beloved *girl*
To the age of *woman*

Online trends and media cling to *girl*
Cool girl, it girl, that girl, dream girl
Whatever the aspirational version of yourself sold back to you is
It usually comes with *girl* on the package

I watch women my age
Go through this unspoken awkward phase
In which *girl* fades away and is replaced
By *woman*
It reads like more than a little language change
As we spend years fighting the way the woman body takes shape
Trying to fit into *girl*
Not understanding why the diet and workout we used to do
Doesn't have the same effect anymore

Everything cool is *girl*
As anti-aging marketing
Says *young is everything!*
In society's fixated fantasy
In which girl is not only sweet and dainty
But girl is *teachable*
Whereas woman is set in her ways
Woman *intimidates*

(Continued)

I hear the dismissive online comments
It's not that deep; this is such a nonissue
Ringing in my ears
That it's *just* a word
But the way we trip over the word *woman*
Carries such a weight that something about it
Does feel heavier to say

I'm Just a ~~Girl~~ Woman

I'm just a conflicted, confused ~~girl~~ *woman*
Who sometimes claims I'm just a girl
Because I am *just a girl*
But I'm so much more than
JUST a girl

Remove the J-U-S-T
Just four little letters
That just seem like hesitancies and redundancies
Or are just included for politeness or niceties
Just like us girls do so often

If it's not needed
~~*Just* delete it~~

And here I am
A girl
A woman
A person
A human
A young heart with a wise mind
Tough skin with a sensitive side
A chaotic disaster with triumphant success
An upside-down mess with right-side-up sense

Stripped down, we are all *just* people
With the inner kids at our cores
Copiloting a compass to this confusing world
But if I shrink myself into the limits of the box
With its four rigid corners spelling out J-U-S-T
JUST attaching to the label
JUST A GIRL is *just* enough
To reinforce the outdated thought
That us girls should live within

(Continued)

The confines of that predefined box
In which our potential is limited
And we are *just* the things expected of us

Shrinking and sinking into the easy-to-define
When we are *just* not *just* a girl
We are a chaotic and harmonious paradox

Girltalk

Do you, like, not like my voice?
Because I would, um, like, totally get that
But, like, why does my vocal fry
My uptalk
And use of filler words
Irk you so much?

Let's, like, be for real
It doesn't even have to be, like, an egregious offense
Like, even a slight, um, overuse of fillers
And a hint of a vocal fry
A bit of uptalk
And end-word extendiiiiing
And I'm dumb
I don't have your respect
And I'm, like,
Not intelligent

But like, did *you* know?
Uptalk is not *just* from women
I've heard mumbling frat-boy accents
And fumbling speeches from leaders who can barely spit out a sentence
But like, why does it seem like the policing and criticism of speaking
Is most commonly directed at women?

Maybe you, like, didn't want to listen to what I have to say anyway
Um, maybe we speak with an open ending to signal softness and friendliness
It's, like, more feminine

(Continued)

And we, like, drag out the words to signal we're, like, not
finished talking
Because we are so used to getting interrupted
And, like, we leave more room for other opinions and
understandings
Filling our sentences with extra language to, like, lighten
Making our messages less, like, direct and certain

Because when the voice is deeper, without space for a question
We're tagged with this harsh, cold unfriendliness
That's too masculine and unattractive

So, like, they say not to
But I reread my emails to make sure my periods don't come
across too strong
And I usually edit a few to exclamation points so no one
assumes I'm rude
And, like, not nice
Because I find that usually earns a warmer response
Even if the writing is, like, less smart

And, like, I've noticed when I *do* speak with clear confidence
that projects my intelligence
Some people react as if it's *too* much
I should relax, dial it back, not be so intense
So I'll keep talking like this
I guess?

I Second-Guessed Everything and Feel Sorry Again

I'm sorry I'm so emotional right now
My period is coming, and I've been feeling so down
I'm sorry if I was a little bit off
And not my typical bright and bubbly self

I'm sorry I've been talking so much
Please feel free to interrupt
I'm sorry for crying about love and stressing over trivial things
When more pervasive problems in the world exist

For feeling the way that I feel
I'm sorry if you've ever been told your pain isn't real
To suck it up, it's not that deep, it's not a big deal

Sorry for wanting to say what I want to say
And do what I want to do
And feel what I want to feel
And be who I want to be
Sorry that I still feel sorry when a woman's pain is not
about survival
But about being free

I'm sorry that I've ever cried over a man when there are
starving children
In our world, our countries, our communities
Sorry that this is the unfortunate truth
Yet others' truths are valid, too

I'm sorry to be confrontational and say
That many realities can occur at once
I'm NOT sorry for experiencing emotions
But I *am* sorry for anyone who has ever been told
To cut the waterworks
And move on

(Continued)

I'm sorry if you think this is out of touch
I'm sorry
I'm sorry that I'm sorry so much

When I Grow Up, I Want to Be a Kid

When I grow up, I want to be a kid
Who never thinks about the texture of their skin
Or spends hours examining their mirrored reflection
To question the harmony or contrast of their face
And whether pictures do too much or too little justice

When I grow up, I want to be a kid
Who fusses over scraped knees
Rather than wrinkles and acne
A kid
Who worries about lost toys, broken crayons, and shadowed monsters in the closet
Rather than wars, rights, and the real-life monsters that people elect into power

When I grow up, I want to be a kid
Who sings along to cartoon stories in which good always wins
Rather than turning on the news to see that evil has taken the lead
A kid
Who swaps playground pebbles as a substitute for money
Rather than trading stocks, spending, and buying in an unstable economy

A kid who wants to grow up to be
A writer
A poet
A teacher
An actress
Without worrying about broken dreams
And being faced with life's realities

(Continued)

When I was a kid
Older is all I wanted to be
Until I reached the inflection point
And now younger is the dream
Because *younger* is pretty
Younger is an oyster of opportunity

When I grow up, I want to be a kid
But the yearning isn't owed to aging or settling in
It's due to the mournful nostalgia
Of the once-colorful, magical world
That I keep trying to re-create
Until the grown-up monsters and adult evils invade
The imaginative brilliance of childhood with their corporate gray

I want to be a kid again, lost in the labyrinth of the grocery store
Rather than an adult lost in the monotony of the office cubicles
Lost then, lost now
But it is the art of the adult that maintains the brightness of
children's worlds
So the young kids like me who dream of growing old
Have the path forward to do so

When I grow up, I want to be a kid
Is that too childish of me to admit?

Mom's Phone Number

One of the first things you do as a baby is reach out your tiny fingers
To get a grasp of the world
So often landing at the friendly fingertips of mom

And how *lucky* I am that I grew up holding her guiding hands
Until one day
My fingers started to slip away
She wanted to keep holding on
But she knew
Her fingers had to slip once, too
So she let them fall
One by one

Watching me ball them up into rage-filled fists
Holding hands with others whose fingers didn't fit
Then wiping the inevitable tears that fell
On the diary page
Making mistakes
Scribbling them out
Writing my own story
Pointing my own way

But just like when I was a baby
My fingers reach to get a grasp of the world
Now riddled with modern chaos and anxiety
The pressure of the future flirts with my nerves

So I dial the phone number of my mother
Sometimes in search of her soothing advice
But other times, it's enough to hear the love in her voice
That echoed through me and guided me to find mine

The Contradiction Confessions Continue

I felt so old at nineteen
Young at twenty-eight
But old again at twenty-three
I was bold at eighteen
Lost in my mid-twenties
And found again by thirty

But that's subject to change
Because when I was younger, I felt old
And now that I'm older, I feel so young
And these twenty-nine *LONG* years have felt so short
As my mind battles with my heart
Between the three a.m. anxious sweats that I've already
    struck all the gold
And the intuitive instinct that I'm a fool to think there's not more

I confess, I'm a contradiction
I know the things I like
I know the things I don't
But I don't have a favorite song
Or color
Or movie
Or artist
Or book
Or a favorite anything—
I change my mind too much

I'm a stubborn Taurus bull
I don't want to be held to anyone's opinion
But I don't care what anybody thinks
Because I know that's a waste of mind space
But I do think
Of what *you* think
Deleting and rewriting

Spending time thinking about how I should care less
Because if the planet is a pebble in the vastness
We're merely tiny grains of sand

I confess
I'm a walking contradiction
I hold a lantern and say *follow my lead*
But when I stay still for a minute
The doubt knots my stomach
And if I know one thing
I know I'll never know
Everything
I know I don't know what I'm doing
And I wonder if I can keep it up
But by some miracle
I keep keeping up

In part, I fear I'm indebted to pure luck
But there *is* skill in thickening the thread I've been hanging on to
Right before it's about to be cut
There *is* talent in the tireless treading of water
To holding my head above the waves
There *is* strength in swimming against the current
To reach the solid land for a gratifying rest in the sun's rays

I'm confident that I'm unsure
But I'm sure I'll have confidence
To find myself wherever I'm lost

Sincerely,
A confident contradiction

I'm NOT Sorry

I'm not going to start by excusing something about my appearance
Saying *I'm sorry*
Don't look at my grown-out recession roots
Or my basic bare-bones broken nails
Sorry, sorry, sorry
I say I don't usually look this way
Even though that's a lie, and I usually do

I'm not going to apologize for still figuring it out
And for not being an expert on everything in the world
I'm not sorry for being proud of myself
And wanting to share my accomplishments with everyone else
I'm not sorry if you perceive that as a big, boastful brag
I put in the work
I'm deserving
I'm not sorry about that

I'm not going to downplay or diminish myself
To seem modest in the acceptable amount
I'm not sorry that sometimes a humblebrag
Is saying it as it is
Because we're all so insecure and flawed
That when one person states they're big
The other might hear their own small

How dare they point out the glaring difference
Shifting blame, it's the other person's fault
Even though we are all big and small and little and large
Maybe we should be looking within and not up and down
    and all around
To gauge where we fall

I'm *not* sorry that I take up space
I'm *not* sorry that I'm proud of myself
I'm *not* sorry if this is irritating, or corny, or cringe
I'm *not* sorry if you didn't like this
Or if you didn't agree
We're all people who exist
And I'm *not* sorry that not only do I want to exist
I want to *live free*

Dandelion Girls

Girls are like delicate flowers
Our pretty petals
So tempting to pluck
To have and to hold

Until we start to grow
In unwanted places
Then we become a pesky weed

A golden dandelion
You can try to get rid of our yellow stains in orderly lawns of green
But we are rooted in resilience
With toughness, we grow and we persist

Our hopeful heads breaking through the sidewalk's concrete
Cracking the thick slabs of ideals and expectations cemented in history
That gray shade poured over the dandelions
Erasure can make a path easy
But we are rooted in resilience
With toughness, we grow and we persist

But dandelions are flowers, too
We are bitter and we are sweet
We are gentle and we are strong
We are bold and we are pretty
And when we do wilt and decay
Our rooted legacy and seeds of resilience
Persist

We are flowers and weeds
We are beautiful disruptions
Slipping and cracking through the sidewalk's concrete
As we dance in defiance
And grow in resistance

Because you can't cement over us
We will always break through

Mirror, Mirror

Dissected to Disgust

Don't worry—
You're not ugly

Dissect your face
With these looksmaxxing tips
Assess your golden ratio
How symmetrical are you?

The tilt of your eyes
The gaps between your teeth
Every inch and centimeter
Makes a bigger difference
Than you would ever think

What kind of nose do you have?
A slim Scandinavian nose?
An Irish nose with the bulb at the tip?
A nose reminiscent of a Grecian goddess?
If so, I'd recommend shaving off some of the bridge

Smooth out your skin
By purchasing these products
Promised to zap away your repulsive zits

Snatch your jawline
By shaving off a bit of your chin

Fill your cheeks
But hollow underneath
So you look skinny
But maintain a youthful essence

Lift the brow
Open the eyelid
File your teeth into vampire points
And pop on perfect bright-white veneers
American Girl doll teeth no more
But don't let us see your bloody bandages
The gruesome horror

The process behind the pursuit of perfection
That society pressures women into
Yet can't forgive them for
The vanity
The obsession

If only she knew how beautiful she was *before* she turned
into a robot
No flaws as proof of humanity
As the tabloids banish her to the valley of uncanny
Exceeding the standard to something much scarier
Manipulating facial features into perfection
So off-putting—
Because this perfection
Was never meant to exist

Another Rat in the Experiment

Face card so lethal
I'd kill for that level of pretty privilege

Red, raw skin from recent exfoliation
Remove the dead skin cells
To stimulate the collagen
Bruised cheekbones from molding and snatching
An angular face

Drain the lymphatic fluids away
Fear the gray
Chop the dead
Brighten the eyes
With a stinging mask
Blue and purple lips swollen
From recent injections

Snatch the waist
Hold—three, two, one
Deepen the lunge

Follow a strict fitness routine
Don't walk—
Run
For Ozempic allegations and legging legs
Ballerina arms reaching to swipe youth's card
On procedures that cement smiles in place

Frozen, I'll look pretty—
A pretty lab rat scampering through a maze
Testing me with the pressures
Of a new experiment every day
A maze designed
Without an escape

Clock In, Lock In, Wake Up, Fear

There's the five-to-nine before the nine-to-five and then the
wind-down five-to-nine
With the biological clock in the back of the mind
Emblematic tick-tock bing-bong ding-dongs
Wake up
To a furious lather and scrub of
Magic potions and mixtures
Luxury lotions and elixirs
On the skin to fight the biggest, longest, everlasting battle
against wrinkles

Lock in
Plug in
Put the headphones in
And run like a girl
Actually, a low-impact
Pricey Pilates class is best
To avoid a droopy old hag *runner's face*

Social media says
Fix up your fatal flaws
The only spiral is you in the mirror
Fumbling your femininity with a wide rib cage
Trying to be deer pretty, but
Oh dear
You're rat pretty, I fear

But remember that none of this is even real
Rat or deer
All are chips in a card game
That's exploiting our faults
To support a larger corporate deal

The Pretty Pills and Their Placebo Effect

Whenever I feel sick of my image
I take a pretty pill
The pretty pills
That I find on the internet for sale

Prescribed by a doctor of glow-ups and pretty privilege
The pretty pills work their makeover magic for a minute

Until another bug comes to infect my immunocompromised
image
And I'm afflicted with the same bout of ugly-girl sickness
The sickness I thought that the pretty pills were fixing

Apparently, *it was all the placebo effect*
I've been taking sugar pills
Feeling better for a little until it wears off
And once again
I need another pretty pill
That only has a surface-level cure

I keep swallowing more pretty pills
Delivered to me from my screen to my ears to my mirror
To keep the pretty-pill industry in business
Making big bucks from my ugly-girl sickness

Copy-and-Paste Faces

Everyone says *no more copy-and-paste faces!*
They say they're sick of the same
Surgically stitched-on stamp
Over a mutilated face

Bring back *real* faces!
At least that's what the caption reads
In an online post with real women's faces
Edited into side-by-side comparisons
With their untouched befores
And plastic afters
Debasing them with a label of unnatural
Confirmed in the comments and in the news

Twenty-two filled with plastic is the new thirty-two
As everyone tears apart each other's faces
There's a forecast for traffic in all lanes of aging

When fed with the request for *real*
The teeth are a bit much
Eyes too far apart
Lips too thin
So the consensus is . . .
Bring back *real faces*
Real, ***pretty*** faces that fit a conventional standard
That people have been trying to reach with surgery
Then wind up in the *copy-and-paste face* enemy territory
As the circus of critics merry-go-round again
Until they can't tell beginning from end

Sleeping Beauty Goes for a Scroll

Imagine if Sleeping Beauty woke up in the modern day
With her weary eyes opening to a phone
Equipped with social media to scroll

In *her* fairy-tale kingdom
She was a beauty for the ages
Her beauty was her name
Her claim to fame

But in *this* modern world
Within only seconds of a curious Instagram scroll
She doubts her beauty, her magic, her self, her soul

The trolls at the castle bridge are still trolls
But now they're in the comments
With their riddles and puzzles
In the form of backhanded glow-up tips
That are repeated by other beautiful princesses
Who introduce themselves with apologies for looking like shit

Between the trolls and the doubtful princesses
Sleeping Beauty lasts mere minutes before she starts to think
How she, too, could be prettier, and what should she fix?

New sounds start to occupy her mind
What to eat to stay thin?
What is heroin chic?
What -core is she?
What aesthetic should she pick?
She buys the promise of fulfillment and beauty
With a simple click
That turns into another click and another cha-ching
Another discovered blemish
Another solution, another fix
Her skin might be smooth glass
But her belief in herself starts to crack

She thought she'd escaped the curses of her medieval home
Only to find she was spellbound by the sneaky evils in her phone

That enchanted her vision
With foggy deception
And led her to doomed obsession
Wishing to trade in the cursed phone
In favor of her nemesis, Maleficent

She'd prefer the *obvious* villain at home

How Old Were You?

Skinny this, skinny that, don't be fat
How old were you when the thoughts on your weight first started to take shape?
Five, six, seven, eight?
Even earlier than that?

I was just a kid
But I still remember standing in line at the grocery store
Trying to read all the magazine covers as fast as I could
My eyes darting to the sneak peeks that hinted at the twisted truth beneath:
Nicole Richie is terrifyingly thin!
Her family and friends are worried!
Allegedly!
Jessica Simpson's diet disaster!
Britney is now bigger than ever!
Beyoncé unveils a better-than-ever slimmed-down figure!

To my little-girl brain
The message was sent, delivered, seen
Skinny this, skinny that
You can be too skinny, but it's better than being fat

From the tabloids and TV to the early years of the internet
The body image virus has grown strongest in our social media apps

Its persuasions spread its skinniness across the web
As its cultlike disciples regurgitate the skinny message
That *every* aspect of your life will be fixed
If you join in listening to them
You're promised to feel free
But there's nothing free about living a life to please

The hunger to be skinny might make you feel light for a little
But it inevitably starts to get heavy
Weighed down by the burdensome thoughts
Of possible pounds lost
That sneak into every meal
Every plan and every interaction
Until every inch of your body

Becomes a massive prison of obsession
With skinny this and skinny that

My Skinny Shack Is Falling Apart

Skinny legend, skinny legend!
What is so legendary about being skinny
When my body is an impermanent thing?
My temporary vessel for being
My home to keep strong and healthy

The foundation to build upon and fill to the brim
With memories, knowledge, stories, and sentimental things
But if I'm always renovating and restructuring
To fit a shallow mold that's later sold
My house will become crowded under constant reconstruction

A loud drill that reverberates through my head
The noise that takes over my thoughts
Because there's *always* more to do
To be the *best* house on the block

Another renovation, then more maintenance
Endless time dedicated to curb appeal
To fit standards that change every few years

Yes, passersby compliment, and it feels so *good*
But it's not that deep warmth that lingers in the bones of the home
It's a shallow joy that lasts on the surface until it collapses in a
light storm
It's an endless fireplace that requires more and more and more

At first, it was about home improvement
But then I was so busy tearing down and fixing
I started missing out on the things that make a house a home
Because a house and a body are impermanent things
And I don't want my legacy to be
How I looked from the street

Daughter Wishes

If I ever had a daughter, I'd wish her life to be so much larger
Than an inch on her waist
The size of her thighs
Some rolls on her belly
Her measures of weight and size

I'd wish she wouldn't spend hours with the mirror,
picking her skin
I'd hope her mind wouldn't be monopolized
By the militant dialogue of calories
And all she needs to burn off as punishment
For eating one too many fries

I'd dream for her brain to be free from a mental tab
Of protein intake and physical activity to track
Those exhausting mental gymnastics that take a tax
With a constant percentage of energy dedicated to skinny math
That turns holidays and dinners and vacations
Into computations and equations on her mass

I'd hope to leave an impression
Deeper than
Scars on the cheeks
Wrinkles on the forehead
Lines around the eyes
Or a blemished body

I'd wish for my impact to be more than my inches and lines
And I'd dream for her to live larger than her pounds and size

Dirty Mirror Did Me Dirty

The more we look at our phones
The dirtier our mirrors become—
And the more screen time we spend
The more our mirrored reflections are clouded

With new labels for our flaws written all around us
The pretty features go foggy
From the steam of the stream
Telling us how to turn up the hotness
With beauty tips like *some light surgery*
As we clean different spots to fixate on
We see the things we need to fill
A fractured image of ourselves reflected in a
Dirty mirror

New words to describe new faults we once didn't know existed
But that get tacked onto the laundry list of all that's wrong
As comment sections of teen boys call gorgeous women *chopped*
Or average, or mid at best
With the next post a slideshow of a natural '90s actress
With the caption to *bring real faces back!*
So which one is it?
Or is it the overexposure to faces and opinions
That dirties the image
Of what beauty even is

Is This What They Mean by Girl Math?

The mathematics of modern beauty
The formula of a feminine face
The instruction for ultimate attraction
With scientifically proven symmetries
That please technological systems

Our social media feeds are ruled by algorithms
What about the human face?

When likes are currency
Views are influence
And following is money
All are measures in the privilege of pretty
Rewarded over and over again

No wonder we're full of criticisms
That reflect sharpest in the mirror
Spitting an image of step-by-step directions for modern beauty
But one miscalculation and the privilege of pretty turns into pity

Up against calculations, robotics on the rise
The physical faults of the person
Battle the technical perfection of AI

Till we are so sickened by its digitized smoothness
That we crave the flaws and bumps of a human face
With warmth, feeling, love, and pain
A depth the computer can't quite replicate

The Beauty Cloud

I love those comparative compliments
From the people who study my face
And interrupt me to say
Did you know you look just like [fill in the blank]?

Some people say I look like one woman
Others argue that's entirely wrong
As they interject to offer their two cents
That I look like a copy of some other someone

It's objective that beauty is subjective
But it's not the *level* of beauty
But the way the eyes of the beholders
So uniquely read my face

I see what I see
But to everyone else
It's a slightly different shape

Like a cloud in the wind
With its fluid definition

Like looking to the sky and seeing a dog
No! Now it's a pig!
Until it all melts together into shades of pink
But whenever *I* try to capture the sunset
The photo never quite does the sky justice
The colors dull down
From what *I* see
Which is different from what *you* see
And you can't quite pin down
The essence of an ever-changing cloud

But What If Our Heads Were See-Through?

I've been drinking ink and eating pages
Snatching my mind in time for summer

Ten thousand words a day to whip my brain into shape
I stretch my vocabulary for extra mind definition
With a twenty-step morning mind routine for cognition
With cerebellum balm and cerebral serum
To avoid those dry thoughts
That smooth the grooves

I drain the propaganda and rot fluids away
So my mind stays plump and young
Once a week, I do a deep cleanse of dead ends and toxins
of thought

I confess, my learnings from last spring no longer quite fit
And I've grown a bit too big for them
So I'm trying to be more intentional with the pen on the page
Rather than my thumbs tapping on the screen
Getting distracted and ditching my mind's fitness routine

I take social supplements and nature vitamins to inspire
and create
Sometimes I intermittent-fast by sitting around and thinking
all day
I'm always productive
So I'll have a pretty brain
A snatched mind that never declines
If you look too long, love will reveal
And you know that phrase they always say
Nothing tastes as good as smart feels

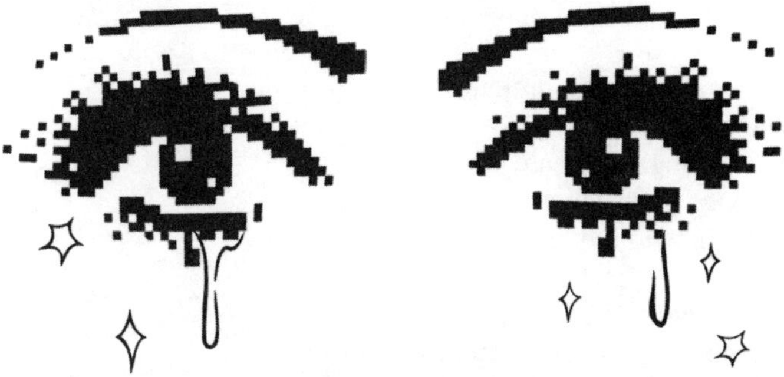

The Land of Make-Believe

Contradiction Nation

We watch Instagram stories of caviar bumps in Shein tops
And buy old-money-aesthetic clothes on Amazon
No seed oils but drugs in the body

Selling quality plastic products
And single-use clothing
Worn as a single-use card of being cool
Swipe *once* on Instagram
Then it's time to move

I'm a contradiction, though
If it consumes you, it consumes me, too
And I like to think I reject things more than I do

I've met those guys, with their gallons of powdered supplements
And rows of sneakers to impress
Who say it's not a big deal
Women aren't treated any less
Ridiculing those blue-haired feminists fighting a system that
No longer exists
But in the quiet, they complain of their loneliness
To a trusted woman who's *apparently* the only willing witness

I live in contradiction nation
Online lives look rich
But addresses say different
We spend our lives wanting to grow up
Until we get an unnatural amount of Botox to look young
We're sick of seeing nepo babies
But social media stars aren't welcome either
I'm not sure who deserves what
But sometimes I see myself when I judge

Contradiction nation doesn't like to plead guilt
And when all lies can be justified
Dirty money is just clean filth

Overconsumption-Core

Get ready with me for another day in the life

Step one:
Wake up
Morning shed
Remove my mouth tape
Silk eye-mask
Face-lifting strap
To reduce my double chin
Clear wrapping mask
To stimulate collagen

Get dressed with me
Starting with my matching pj's
Run, don't walk
Quick, add them to cart

Try on three outfits—
All linked
And I just redid my closet
Because I'm a bright spring
And the beige didn't complement my skin
Care routine
Starting with sunscreen
I have seven tubes
But there's only one brand I religiously use
And my recently microneedled and tretinoin-lathered skin
Can't handle the sun

Anti-aging
Anti-aging
Anti-aging
Isn't it fun?
Please
How old do I look?
Do I still look young?

(Continued)

Come along
On my grocery shopping vlog
All new vitamins—
The glow comes from within
But suddenly
There's a voice in my head

What about that subscription of vitamins you already have?
The monthly boxes are piling up
Half expired
And what about the chlorophyll water?
That green, minty flavor
I don't think I've touched since 2021
And what about slugging?
Do I even remember what that was?

I open my phone
That voice in my head
Stops
To welcome in a stream of collective questions
That draw on my impulses
As I try to purchase my way into fitting in

What's the aesthetic of the month?
Shoe of the summer?
New hair color?
New shampoo?
Drop your links
Lather
Rinse
Repeat
Repeat
Repeat
Reread

Which Illusion Are You?

The illusion of choice
What's your aesthetic?
What's your vibe?
What box do I put you in?
What kind of girl are you?

Are you a rock star girlfriend?
A mob wife?
A clean girl?
An e-girl?
Are you a manic pixie dream girl?

How about a Tumblr girl?
A 2014 girl?
A coconut girl?
A VSCO girl?

Coastal grandmother?
No
Coastal cowgirl
Actually
You're an eclectic grandpa
Girl

Light academia?
Dark academia?
Ballet-core?

I'm going to the salon
What kind of nails should I do?
Red nails?
Red-nail theory
Blue nails?
Blue-nail theory
No

(Continued)

Pink nails
Pink-nail theory
Or glazed doughnut
No, no, no
Blueberry-milk nails

I *need* new makeup
Should I go to Ulta or Sephora?
I *need* my hair done
Should I do old-money bronde?
Or a Scandinavian hairline?
No
A butter blond
Or
A copper cowgirl red

Where should I buy all my clothes?
The store with four dollar signs?
Three dollar signs?
Two dollar signs?
One?

What are the odds they're made in the same factory?
And that all these aesthetics
And boxes
And niches
We want to put ourselves in
Are a facade of choice
To create an illusion of control
Even though at the center
It's all the same -core

I Think I'm Turning Plastic

Welcome back to *another* day in the life
First, I take off my plastic, then put on my plastic
Then plastic my plastic to microplastic

Get in my gas
Order a plastic
Gas to the plastic place to get plastic

So overconsumption-core
Consumerism- and convenience culture–coded
Money might make the world go round
But will it also collapse our home's ground?

Drowning under a billion tons of greed
As plastic replaces the fish in the sea
The water in our streams
The blood in our veins

Fossil fuels fill up the air we breathe
As fresh air becomes a luxury
A luxury that I'm sure will be repackaged in plastic
Flown across the world
And sold back to me

As the plastic production
Plastic-wraps the planet
With a warming skin
That scorches mine
The damage and chemicals
That pollute my pretty
With ugly wrinkles

(Continued)

Pretty plastic faces, pretty plastic products, and pretty plastic lives
Flash thousands of times in front of *low-income white-girl eyes*
Or *siren eyes*
Or *fox eyes*
Or *negative canthal tilt eyes*
The viral label doesn't matter
So long as they stay glued to the selling stream

They say the difference isn't made
By *one* individual
It's the corporations at fault

They're right; it's not *us* to blame
But if enough hands point fingers together
We command their demand
And mold their plastic profit
Into a better shape

The Fast Lane Just Got Faster

In a world of *fast*
Fast fashion
Fast food
Fast trends
Fast media
Fast living
Fast dating
Fast feelings

Be **s l o w**
We aren't hardwired for the fast processing speeds
That have set the modern pace for society
Where being busy and productive
Is an essential part of our worth
No time to rest
They say to sleep when we're dead
It's all about faster, production, birth

More, more, more
We mustn't exceed our designated time
Approved to mourn

As the machine routine glitches our natural systems
With incompatibility warning messages
That alert us to the fast living demands
For hyperproductivity
To make fast money
That feeds the fires of fast
That are burning us alive
And depleting our systems
Of the resources we need to survive

(Continued)

The fast lane is too fast
Too long
Too lonely
But if we *have* to go fast
Does anyone want to carpool instead?

I'm Over the Over-ness of It All

Everything is *over* the top
Like the water *over*head
After jumping *over*board
Off a sinking ship

Diving into an *over*consumption of media
That has us *over*exposed to our own flaws
And the things we like and things we don't
And the beautiful things and the ugly things
And the heartfelt hope and the devastating doom
But mostly doom and then more doom

*Over*exposed to things we need and the things we lack
Lending to *over*spending on material things that are
    *over*promised to be
Absolutely life-changing!

*Over*exposed to dating options, advice, and theories
That have us *over*analyzing *over*generalized therapy speak
And holding so much space for our boundaries
That there's no space left to genuinely connect

Exposed to SO much
Have we lost touch?
With our own feelings and instincts?

Maybe I'm *over*dramatic
Or *over*whelmed
Or *over*stimulated
Or maybe I'm just *over* the *over*-ness of it all

Turn the Present into Profit

They say *there's no time like the present*
But the present moment doesn't present as a gift
When it feels like
There's no free time
And no time is free
When there's no time to breathe

News breaks
And without the skip of a heartbeat
Or the deep draw of a breath
For a satisfying sigh of relief
The movie is already being made
With billion-dollar studios fighting over the rights
To pay the most coin
For the current disastrous headline

Like a horrifying mass murder
The collective nation grieves
But before the tears dry
They're being milked for money

They say *there's no time like the present*
To battle rivals, swords sharpened
Cutting throats for the biggest bounty
That doesn't glint with integrity

The Land of Make-Believe Has Monsters, Too

I can dye my hair pink and try on a new identity for a week
I can rearrange, inject, and change my face
Sculpt my stomach and read quoted excerpts
But if these are the only things that change
Does it change my fate?

I've fallen into a modern obsession with surfaces
And barely scratching them
With thin veils over nuanced concepts
I can see there's more, but I'm scared to lift them

Because I like living in the Land of Make-Believe
It's less chaotic, more enchanting
Although somehow, the monsters I've met in real life still find
  a way in
When I can no longer ignore the rapidity
With which my snow globe of a safe place starts to shake
Until my utopian, aesthetic Land of Make-Believe
Breaks

And I fall deep into the cracks
Of the surfaces I barely scratched
Forced to lift my protective veil
From my pretty, aesthetic pink hair

What Radicalized You?

I never found anything *radical*
About the lyrics to “Colors of the Wind”
Or the plot of *A Bug’s Life*

I find it a shame that these *normal, moral* beliefs
Or having an opinion and speaking it with grace
Shifts you into being a *radicalist*

I thought we were all rooting for good to win
That Lord Voldemort
And President Snow
Were the evil villains we agreed to root against

I recognize how radical this statement might seem
Like our nonfiction villains are of the same dramatic caliber
As these fictional monsters who plow tyrannical paths to power
With racial discrimination
And media manipulation
And extreme class division
On second thought
Maybe it’s not such a radical comparison, after all

So if you were to ask what radicalized me
It’s not these stories and movies that make moral sense

It’s the groups of men who all look and walk the same
That talk about the health of *me* and *my* body
And how it impacts *them*
As they talk bills and laws
Without the input of women

Or when a woman with salon-bleached blond hair
Who *never* dares
To allow a shadow of a root
Looks at me through the TV screen with her full, thick,
    perfected lashes
As her freshly filled and blushed lips say she can't believe the
    cost of eggs
Who can afford these grocery prices?
She says
It's ridiculous
As she flashes her three-carat diamond engagement ring

My *radical* eyebrows can only stay lifted so long
So I unlock my phone for a midnight distraction
Scrolling through
Propaganda, beauty tips, conspiracies, fitness routines
Footage of aliens, influencer beef, sparks of a revolution
With people on the same side arguing the proper way to start
And the *correct* way to deal and cope

Just around the radical riverbend
Maybe the frustrated tears will merge together
Into a unified sea that waves with hope
Powered by the moral *sense* that radicalized us

This Isn't About Cubes of Ice

Day in the life
Of watching the world end through a phone screen
I'm sorry; I apologize
Is that overdramatic fearmongering?

I fear the fear isn't good for the skin
The cortisol increases facial puffiness
They say to reduce inflammation with an ICE bath for the face
With a rush of blood and the shocking violence of the cold ICE
You'll look younger, glowier, pores tight

Force out the *repulsive* impurities
Eradicate those scary stains on an otherwise perfect face
For the promise of a prettier life
Just like the celebrities on the screen
Except they say it's just ICE baths, products, extra support from
  injectables
And that's all it will ever be

But it's a lie; it's not just ICE
It's more invasive surgery

The kind that doesn't allow for recovery
Before the next
Get ready with me
That details the wake-up
The workout
The clock-in
The lock-in
The makeup
Till I scroll

Then I bed rot
I crash out
Watching families be ripped apart
And a podcast clip that implies that
Empathy is political now?

So I distract myself
With some reality TV
That is an escape from reality
Ironically

Don't talk about it, don't talk about it
Capitalism doesn't like that
Put on your mouth tape
And just stay quiet!

But I don't want to trade my voice
For the richness of the silence
Because that's not worth much

Rubber Bullets

In the Land of Make-Believe
The bullets are rubber

And the leader of the land
Told us an army helps to protect the pure
With bullets always at the ready
They say not to worry
They're only made of rubber

The rubber
That's imported from another
Even though the leader of the Land of Make-Believe
Says anything from anywhere else is
A TERRIBLY, HORRIBLY
HORRIFYING
TOTALLY
NOT
EMPHASIS ON NOT!
BEAUTIFUL THING!!!

There's no logic in the Land of Make-Believe
Our leader would say that's a BIG, BEAUTIFUL THING
Because if logic existed here
Endless imports of rubber bullets
Would make the costs grow higher
At least according to our leader's laws
And aloud preying, preaching thoughts

So we keep burning the rubber till the wheels spin out
As we drift into oncoming traffic
And cause a headfirst collision that impacts us all
No matter what side you're sitting on in the car

Like so many others
I *tried* to swerve away from the disaster
But I remember waking up with this sinking feeling on the 6th of November
When I saw our new driver
Who's cashing in on the ride for their own gain and personal rise
And no matter what the advertisement says on the outside of the car
The leader of the Land of Make-Believe doesn't care if the passenger lives or dies

My Mind Is a Gold Mine

When there is no land left
To buy, level, and brand
They will come for our attention spans
Paving over the grooves in our brains
That make for valuable advertising space
And profitable commercial real estate

The business venture already seems to be well underway
As they progress on their objective
To create a monocultural society
In which we all fall somewhere
On one of two sides of a horseshoe diagram
In which each side believes they couldn't be more distant
Unaware that there are as many similarities as differences
But no matter the arguments, it's all in the name of data

Sorted into preferential factions
That trigger which ads
Should be layered into each person's apps

It's all going according to plan
With planted programming
That plays with our joy receptors
And emotional processing centers
That give us a boost and hit
And grow into an addiction
That keeps us coming back

Raising generations with technology dependence
For *everything*
Socializing, working, thinking

Our attention harvested
Like pigs on a farm
Feeding us advertisements
That live in our subconscious
But rather than roaming fields of green
Our data is roaming
In new places with new preferences
That train an algorithm
That controls what we see
And convinces us of what we need
Under an illusion of luxury
That sells a belief
This is what it is to be free

It's the new frontier!
They dug all the gold and diamonds
From the earth
Now they're mining our minds
As the next capitalist resource

The Attention Economy

Welcome to the attention economy!
In which the most prized possession is *your* attention
That's swindled out of you
With rage-bait selling tactics

People will say anything so long as you don't scroll away
Because your seconds of attention are what gets them paid
As people spill *piping hot tea*
And share ambiguous content and claims
That open the door for the kind of speculative arguing
That lights the matchstick of hate
That was waved in front of your face

Which then spreads like wildfire across online feeds
Fueled by the winds of extremist hate
And a human bias toward negativity

The only problem is that the fire burns out quick
In this ruthless battle for relevancy
Where concentration is the most coveted currency

In the attention economy
It doesn't matter if that money is dirty
As long as the ashes build up to the next attention-grabbing
controversy

Until the audience is so burned-out that they don't care about
anything
Except for digging through the slop in search of something more
nutritious
That is more worthy of the price of their precious attention

An Attention Intermission

Oh, you're still here?
By now, I half expected you to be gone
Not because I don't believe in my own intrigue
But because attention spans have been so whittled down

Fed with bits and pieces of content
And every convenience at the fingertips
I thought you might have given in
To your distraction screen instead

I understand
I took a scrolling intermission while writing this
And maybe you're just getting back from yours

So if you've made it this far
I appreciate your riches of attention
And for paying me with your focus of gold
For your next attention intermission
If you decide to hit social media
Don't forget to shower me
With your gems of likes
Fortune of follows
Funds of tags
And precious jewels of reposts

Thank you for spending your attention on me!
I hope it's worth it
Because you can't return it

Do You Like My Pretty Pixels?

Pixels of me, pixels of you
To you, I'm made of pretty little pixels
1,080 by 1,920 to be exact
At a vertical nine-to-sixteen aspect ratio
For optimal viewing
Of a pixel-perfect life
With pixel-perfect skin
And pixel-perfect hair
And pixel-perfect things

Creating an idealistic image of what our reality should be
Trapped by the pixels in our screens
Fragmented fractions of our full selves
Gracing social media
To make a lasting digital impression
That informs perception
Are my pixels pretty enough for you?

Do the electromagnetic signals of my sound
Wave in a way that captures your attention
For enough seconds to make me a viral sensation?

Kafka's Metamorphosis *Meets a Modern Girl*

I woke up today to find myself transformed into a robot
Yesterday was just another formulaic *get ready with me*
Day in the life
Step by step
Performing my rigid morning routine
Straight from a TikTok titled
Hot Girl's Guide to Success: The Morning Ritual Recipe

For my outfit of the day
I've been recently trying to find my personal style
So I scrolled through social media for a while
And came across the latest trend to go viral

I didn't have any immediate thoughts or feelings
I scrolled reactions and assessed the most popular takes
That informed my mind on how to feel and what to say
Which came in handy when I repeated verbatim an opinion
    I saw online
As if it were mine
When I was asked about it later that day
Good thing I scrolled
Because my own opinion could have been too out-there or niche

Especially because I learned recently
That what I thought were personality quirks
Was actually a *DSM-5* diagnosable mental illness
More bugs in my system I'll have to pay to fix

I didn't feel it happening
I didn't feel the undefinable edges of my personality
    and human identity
Slowly being massaged and molded by media and algorithms
To fit into this four-point classifiable body

(Continued)

As if I'm made up of keywords that can be searched
To direct to an exact copy of me for purchase
In one click, it's so convenient

And now that I'm a robot
I'm incompatible with humanity
And nobody can connect with me

I just wanted to fit in and fix my wrongs
But now I compute the challenges of being human
As a better battle than being a lonely robot

The Authenticity Trials

Am I on trial?
Are you the jury?
Assessing my authenticity
To come to a verdict of whether or not
My personality *seems* authentic enough

Being rated as internet-authentic-approved is a complex case
With the bulk of evidence gathered through a screen
But when only what is shared is what is seen
It's hard to rule on a person's authenticity

Before the authenticity trials begin
There's first the court of cringe
In which an overexuberance is examined against an order
 of nonchalance
To ensure authenticity requirements are referenced
 and checked off

To win, you have to be yourself
But in the balanced amount
That isn't boring
But not *so* energetic
That it seems performative
And is interesting and timely enough
That it appeals to the majority
With the *acceptable* amount of palatable personality
That doesn't translate as too watered-down

The laws of the land
Request a strategy for authenticity
So my defense is that this request
Is a complete violation of self
I cite the policing of authenticity
As a marker of morality
To be pointless
When we are all performing to some degree

I Dressed My Life as an Aesthetic, but I Still Felt the Same

Spend a day with me as a New York City influencer
Rolling out of my gifted bedsheets to my top-of-the-line
alarm clock
That simulates the first peek of the sun
Because the real one barely breaks through the concrete to
my high-rise
If I want better natural light
I have to pay
It crosses my mind
But the partnerships have been slower these days

I get ready for seven a.m. Pilates after rubbing luxurious creams
and serums on my eyes
That drift down to the passersby
Beneath the floor-to-ceiling windows of my high-rise
A city of strangers walks by
Everyone who knows me lives online

I can't complain
This job is easier than my last nine-to-five
I share the glamorous bits of life
The highlights that get me high

I say I'm *so* obsessed
In a photo dump from the party with the girls
With the caption *they are my heart and soul*
But they keep forgetting where I went to school

My phone pings all day and night
I feel so alone
So I change my hair and my aesthetic
But it doesn't change a thing
Like I'm the only living girl in New York
But I'm a character *acting*
Not a person living

And I got so far from home
I can't remember where I started

I think I ate up my own numbers so fast
I lost my appetite
Starving
I pack my designer bags
Catch the next train
Hopping off when my old soccer field blurs green on my right
I smell the cows in the field behind the house
There's no AC
It's only May
But it's already sticky

I forgot my silk pajamas
So I slip on my college tee from 2018
Grab a mismatched glass from the old wood cabinet
And twist the plastic spigot of the boxed red wine

Not the trendiest aesthetic by social media's design
But it's the most my cup has been full in a long time
Even though it's not filled with New York City's
Most exclusive supper club's fancy wine

Subject of My Own Satire

At the end of a doomscroll
I accidentally fell into my screen
In search of chaotic content to inspire me
My bungee cord severed from the outside world
I found myself caught in the current of the online void

Swimming in the ebbs and flows of views and likes
The blue light was keeping me up at night
Checking the analytics like the weather
To see if I'd been cast by the algorithm
Into the shadows
Flopping in the water
Drowning in the sea
Of oversaturated content
Overstrategizing my way out of it

I became the subject of my own satire
The one I warned about
Since then, I still dive in
But I don't obsess over the swim to success
I just float

Less Likes, More Love

I was driving down the highway
When my eyes were drawn to this trippy graffiti billboard
With the words
Less likes, more love

I didn't catch a sponsor or a brand
Just *less likes, more love*
Spelled out in an airbrushed heart

I wondered if we've stepped such a significant distance
From our heart's humanity, purpose, and reason
That we need such reminders
Not to grow too used to the anonymous online hearts
And their yummy social currency
That we forget the taste of true connection

Not to get too addicted to the sugar we use as a vice to soothe
    our minds
That we *lose* our minds over a temporary fix
And an easy dose of convenience
That satiates us *just* enough
So we don't have to face the challenges of the real thing

So much so that this bright, bold message
Was plastered on a highway high above my head

Less likes, more love
More love, less likes

Healthy Content Diet

You need to go on a content diet
Stop overconsuming empty calories
On a mindless doomscroll binge
That fills your brain to the brim
With low-quality, high-speed media
That constipates your creativity
Inflames your emotions
And makes your mind all foggy

Oversaturated media of low substance *might* be addicting
But it leaves you with that heavy, sluggish feeling
Consuming too much information in one sitting
Is hard for the brain to break down and digest

So I suggest you try a content diet
Be more intentional and feed yourself
With higher-quality programming that is easier to process

Moderate your social media intake
I promise you'll feel so clear and light every day

If you want to be hot, you have to be fit
By working out the muscle of your mind
Stretching words, lifting pages
Fighting off lazy content persuasions
You *need* to find a healthier content plan
Your brain is *begging* for those critical nutrients

Happily Ever After, Ever?

My Love Life According to Rotten Tomatoes

My heart is hopeful!
Why wouldn't it be?
With the access to love in the internet age
All the swipes, searches, connections at my fingertips
Swiping through people as potential romantic comedy plots
I can tell from the poster and the one-sentence synopsis
When one of the options is so predictable
That it wouldn't be worth watching

But sometimes
I still press play
Just to fill the space
Some background noise, a good distraction
And to my surprise, I find myself
Unusually invested and paying attention

Until there comes an inevitable miscommunication
Or risky jumping in
For the plot
And unlike the ambitious melodramatics of soppy stories
 on the plasma screen
At the first inkling of inconvenience
The plot of a real-life modern romance
Usually does not advance from this

Because in moments of discomfort
And uncertain risk
There's easy access to less-complicated options
In a couple more swipes and clicks

We live in the ultimate era of connections
Yet struggle to deepen any of them
Experiencing a momentary high
Consuming love like it's scrolling for content

My Theory Is That Not All Theories Apply

A social media theory is all that you need
Like red-nail theory to achieve red-string theory
But sometimes the string is invisible
In theory
Or you might come to find
There is no string at all
As you come up on the three-month rule
When, according to taxicab theory
Your situationship's occupancy light wasn't on

If you happen to come across each other again
It must be meeting-twice theory
Second time's the charm

But when the situationship starts pushing three months
There comes the familiar stress
As you wait for a text that you never get

The algorithm slowly tailors to you
As you spiral and assess
If the root of your failed love is because
Your attachment style is anxious
Theorizing which relationship theory
To theoretically apply to your life
Which dating theory, in theory
Is to blame
In a never-ending texting game?

Analyze, spiral, scroll
Validate how you feel
The theory is that this social media fixation of dating
Is making the process even worse
But that's just one theory
Theoretically
In theory, of course

The Plague of Social Media Advice

The internet is a host
For viruses
Infectious misinformation
Pathological posers
And a bad-advice parasite
With a prescribed one-size-fits-all treatment

Have you been prescribed dating advice?
Like *if he wanted to, he would*
When we're lovesick, we reach for comfort
But this cozy blanket of bad advice
Is riddled with holes

Have you caught an infection from *those* contagious theories of love?
They prey on the immune system being down
Then make your head ache
With thoughts you didn't consider before
Prolonging your symptoms of heartbreak more

Be wary of the doctors with phony credentials who claim expertise
Because they benefit from the sickness
And might sink you further into your disease
Watch where you go with a fresh wound on your heart
The internet might be a toxic place for you to be

Graveyard of Ghosts and Exes

Instagram stories are a graveyard of ghosts
Haunting the views and likes
An ex silently watches
After years of not talking

Are we supposed to believe this is romantic?
Posting an Instagram story and scrolling through
To make sure that *one* someone—
An old flame, or a lingering ghost—
Clicked a mini digital bubble of you?

Will the next generation of love poems
Detail thirst traps
And social apps
And DMs?

Flirting through hearts on stories
If you're lucky, a slide up that's more than the auto-response
emojis
The thrill of waiting till the last hour to view a twenty-four-
hour story

There's nothing romantic about it
But it pains me to admit
That I can't say I haven't felt this, too

The Playbook of Love

The Playbook of Love
Is marketed as an easy read
With straightforward romance strategies
Its highlights are lifted from the page
To the phone, to the screen, to friends, to the internet feed

As the playbook's inescapable rules and theories
And repetitive viral strategies
Are drilled into everyone's heads
Lovers exchange interactions with pressured evaluations
From takeaways of a *red flags versus green flags* list
Rather than feeling the feelings and going off-script

I think the Playbook of Love is a sham
That keeps us enveloped in its pages
On a never-ending mission to find the real thing
Until the demand is for perfection
And we overanalyze everything

So caught up in the ideas and rules
That your lover forgets to be them
And you forget to be you

Are we all missing the fine print
That the Playbook of Love
Isn't meant to be on the bestseller list?

His Type Is Robot, I Fear

His type isn't *girl*
His type is robot
I fear

The kind of girl who enjoys watching the game
While throwing back a couple beers
But never too many that it's unruly
And she's never concerned about the calories
Because she's programmed to be naturally thin

She's electric and lights up every room she walks into
She dazzles and shines
But in a way that doesn't take away from him
She's interesting
But never more interesting than him

She has an easy pregnancy
She's like a machine
She is naturally good at mothering
She's never tired or exhausted
It's like she never runs out of batteries
And you wouldn't believe
The way her slim figure bounced back so quickly

Yet it's not that she doesn't have any flaws
She does
But in a way that feels manufactured
Like a robot
So her baggage is designer
Not too much
Just enough to develop her character

(Continued)

And every so often it's written into the code
That she gets a pimple on the tip of her nose
And he'll call her Rudolph and make jokes
And she'll laugh along and say
I know

She constantly upgrades
Her nails are always done
Her hair is naturally blond
As she ages, she still looks young
But it's all natural
She's not plastic
He thinks less of women who do *all that crap*
Which is ironic
Because his type is robot
His type isn't even real
I fear

Tragic Single Woman

Little girls dream of weddings in their white princess dresses
Playing with their baby dolls in their pink plastic kitchens

The dream life of the mother and wife
The princess gets her prince
The romantic happy ending

Raised to raise
Birthed to birth
Loved to love
And if not
They say *there must be something wrong*
To make her so *unworthy* of love

For so long
There was no respect for alternative plots
Often there's still not
Because when we see an older single woman
Most people assume
That it's not out of her *want*
They repeat
Something must have gone wrong

Because if I say
I want to be a bachelor
When I'm older and single
With no kids
I wouldn't be a successful bachelor
I'd be a sad *old maid*
Even if that's what I *wanted* to be
It's not what we think of when we think of a fairy tale
It's a single-old-woman tragedy

Can You Please Delete That Memory of Me?

I want to snatch the locket with the picture of me off his neck
The one snapshot he took from the first and only time we met
An image that tenses my chest
And hangs high in my head
Framed as ugly embarrassment

Over how I positioned myself
Stumbling over empty words
Because I couldn't get his perception out of the way
A self-inflicted paper-cut of shame
From the flat picture I portrayed

Shame that's turned into frustration
Over the rare unflattering portrait
Captured in his locket
As I wish to unlock it
To modify and edit

I obsess over the what-ifs of the future I've conjured
up in my head
What if one day someone mentions my name
Or I come across his screen
So he scans his memories
To find that unsavory headshot of me?

But when I was first in the haze of the flash
The film of his kisses still fresh
The impression felt vivid
With few flawed vignettes

Now, after days of quiet distance
I've found myself scratching a fixation
Of the minor vignettes that went wrong
As my propensity for the negatives
Has me staring at the memory so long
That I've distorted reality and invaded my own past

I've projected *my* insecurities
Into an imaginary locket that hangs on *his* chest

He Ghosted Me

We're both a 45-degree Saturday morning
With marbled clouds overcasting a gray hue
But you're in November
And I'm in April
At first glance of fresh, groggy eyes
We flock together
But I'm in a different season of life
And after a few blinks
I see the truth

I planted and watered our seeds
But you dried and dropped dead leaves

I was ready to wrap you in my golden sun
But you were cooling off as I was warming up

I hoped our flowers would grow
But you iced our common ground
Bitten by your sudden frosty chill
Without even a whistle of wind
I woke up to your silent snow

I showered the earth with teardrops
But after some storms my flowers still came up
And everything turned green once again

I could see so clearly
As you remained so cloudy
Stuck in your November day

I'll pass through you again soon
And I'll say thank you
For the blossoms that bloomed out of the wounds

The Fluffy White Caterpillar

When I was little, I remember playing in my driveway
When a fluffy white caterpillar inched toward me
I thought the caterpillar could use a touch of color
So I took my pastel chalk and colored it rainbow
The next day
I woke up
With an itchy red rash all over my skin
As it turns out
The fluffy white caterpillar
Was poisonous

I've met unassuming caterpillars just like this
On dating apps, turned to dinners and nights
For a little while, I see it as it is
Until I get caught up
Adding my own color again

Painting them to be something they're not
And just as when I was a little girl
The hopeful habit ends in hopeless hurt

The irritating itches of the bumpy red rash
Are now knots that fill my stomach with
The kind of anxious discomfort that can't be scratched

So these days
I've been watchful of white caterpillars
And where I place my chalk

Should I Move Out West?

I've looked in the shadows of New York skyscrapers
Waited on the steps of brick Boston brownstones
I've wished on the fallen petals of cherry blossoms
And hoped for footsteps in the country snow

I've searched far and wide
All across the East Coast
Packing up, settling in, moving on
I've collected hauntings and ghosts

There were moments of home in someone else
But the walls weren't strong enough
I lived far too long in the ruins after it fell
So now I can't tell
If it was ever built on love

An undying story of romance I've been told
In fairy tales and songs with lyrics that live in my bones
From muscle memory, I've repeated those exchanges of words
But every time I look back, I recall the feelings as skeletal

I've been held
I've said it all
I've been adored
But I'm still searching for confirmation in my soul
That my person is real and not a fantasy I was sold

I hear the booming business of love
My sight cuts through its fallacies
With my eyes glued to the show
Of performative confessions and heartfelt spending
But I can't deny that hope still lives in my bones
For my own happily-ever-after ending

So I'll keep looking in the skyscrapers, the brownstones, the
blossoms, and the snow
And if I never find the other end of my hope
I have faith that the lessons of the quest will still nurture my soul

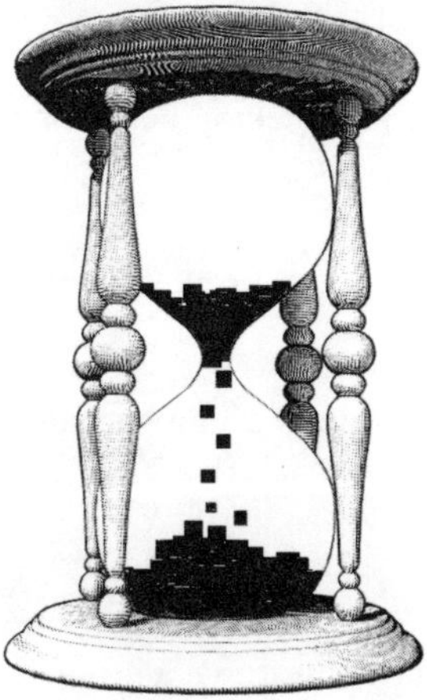

Disenchantment

Dancing in the Club of Desperation

I'm dancing in a club of desperation
Surrounded by the scents of suffering

The girl next to me keeps checking her phone
And scanning the room
Desperate for a text
Desperate for a look
Desperate for love

The guy at the bar is putting it all on his card
Desperate to be liked
Desperate to be seen
Desperate for love

The bouncer at the club turns down a group
He whispers to the other that there was room
Desperate for power
Desperate for respect
Desperate for love

I'm dancing in a club of desperation
Desperate to dance
Desperate for fun
Desperate for love

I'm dancing in my room, and I'm dancing alone
I'm dancing with my friends, and I'm dancing with you
You're grabbing my waist
Desperate for that look on my face

But for me it's not in you, and for you it's not in me
Because love is in the rhythm, and love is in the beat
And love is in the lyrics, and love is in the tune

Sometimes I do get lost in that euphoric sound
But other times
I forget
And find myself spending too much time looking around
Because ignorance is bliss
When you're dancing in a club of desperation

I'm a Busy Bee

There's this constant competition to out-busy each other
I'm sorry—I've been so busy
Oh yeah—me too, so busy—
So booked and busy

At this point of the exchange
I'm now going to explain
My busyness
Step by step
And imply
That not only am I busy—
But I'm busier than you
As if there is this underlying respect that comes from being
The busiest bee
Buzzing—
Even in circles
Around the room

So stay busy
Or get out of the hive
Says the queen bee
The message trickles down the hierarchy
To the worker bees
To the drone bees
Be busy, my busy bees
Soon becomes a competition of who can be
The busiest bee

But I remember
Only the queen bee gets the royal jelly
While my wings are stuck
In the sticky thick
Of production

Dreaming of floating to a different colony
The queen bee says I'll never survive
Alone—
Outside the business of the hive

But one day I separated from the swarm
And fell asleep among the flowers
Peering over the petals to see
I was indeed
Left behind

I thought I'd never stay alive
But I stumbled upon other lost bees
Aimlessly buzzing
Just like me
And we created our own hive
In which our busyness wasn't business
But finding a new purpose
Beyond serving the competition

Forfeiting—
To taste the fruits of our labor
The honey is richer
When we're harmoniously humming together
Spending more time among the flowers
To savor the sweetness of life

Ribbon Tales of Perfection

I've stumbled into a ribbon hyperfixation
An obsession adorning me from hair to toe
With the expectation that the trending loops of lace
Tie neatly into a pristine
Perfect bow

If the ends are tattered
I cut the tangled threads
If the loops are asymmetrical
And don't strike the best balance
Between the tight knot at the core
And the bouncy tails that come to an ever-so-slight upward curl
I retire or retie
With shinier ribbon
Again and again
Until I reach
Perfection

Then I plaster them all over everything
But as all my hyperfixations do
My obsession eventually flips
And the repetition makes me sick

Now I can't bear to look at the boring bows
With their obnoxious excellence
And flawless ribbons
Slapping me across the face
Dispelling me from a perfectionist chase

I'm starting to favor
The wonky bows
With uneven ends
And funky patterns
That accept their tatters

Although you might wish I would
I won't tie this into a neat bow
Please accept the loose ends
And follow the hanging threads
Tying your unique version instead

The Hourglass

Time is running out!
Sprint, don't run!
Purchase these products
Before they're gone!

Time is running out!
On my youthful, glowy face
As I go to extremes to anti-age!

Time is running out!
My biological clock ticks down
The second hand says
My juvenile days of freedom and fun
Are done
You're thirty?
It's time to settle down!

The rhythmic ticking of the clock
Rings in the back of my head
Watching the sands of the hourglass pass
I feel every grain
That changes state
From future
To past
And with each grain
There's less living left
As I become buried beneath
The mountain of anxiety
Building at the base of the hourglass

On an impulsive whim
I take the hourglass
And crack its fragile glass
My fear falls to the floor

And for a moment—
Time is flat
I can't tell
The future from the past
Between what slipped through the floorboard cracks
And what I swept into the trash

Without the shadow of the building mountain of the past
The trance of the ticking goes quiet
And each moment
Moves forward with music instead
At last
Released from the sinking quicksand
That trapped me into a prison
Of the pressures in my own head

Time is passing; that's a fact
But time will pass faster
If I'm obsessed with watching the hourglass

Dreams and Nightmares

I followed a dream, and I hated it
I walked up the daunting steps to success
Took the jump without the safety net
And hiked all the way up
To the idyllic castle at the top

I lived there for a while
And told the watchers
This was the life that I loved
But I started to notice cracks in the castle walls
At first, I didn't want to admit
But it wasn't the dream that I'd thought

For some time, I got caught in the minds of others
What would everyone think?
If I retreated back down the failure steps
The *I told you so*s multiplied in my head

But once the cloud of others' judgments cleared
I looked to the left, and a different dream appeared
A dream that never would have been revealed
If I hadn't pulled at the first dream's threads
And trekked my way up that first set of steps

I chased a dream, and I hated it for a bit
Until my path redirected me to the next
Unimaginable thing
Which is how we got here
As I write and you read this

My dream that made it to print

Glitching Out

I'm glitching out
I need a factory reset
My phone is in my hand
But my body has become a device
Programmed to operate
According to code
Talking to my keyboard with the manufactured thought
That I'm the one in control

Systems checking all the boxes
Programmed to keep processes operating
But I think I'm downloading a virus
I've been experiencing sensory overload

Because my heart isn't hardware
My intelligence isn't artificial
My soul isn't a technical system

They got greedy, and I'm short-circuiting
Overriding their control
I need to deprogram
And reprogram
With rawness and realness
To strip away the safety of the network
For a scary second
And reconnect
With my nature, my flesh

Silence Is a Scarier Sound

My head has been ringing with
Headline after headline after headline
After breaking-news headline

But I think the sound of silence is much scarier
Than the constant ping of my email
Or slew of thrown-together words from politicians
Regurgitated on social media
As a mishmash of mediocre dissections

But it's the spaces *between* the words
The moments *between* my notifications
Those *silent* moments
That make my heart beat faster

Like when I lie in bed at night
Just me, alone, in the darkness
When my mind wanders to a weird place
And rather than counting sheep
I tune in to the nebulous silence
My heart pounding to its energetic static

I reach for the light of my phone
To illuminate the dark corners
I turn on *any* sort of noise
White noise
Brown noise
Green noise
Ocean waves
Forest sounds
Meditation music

Sometimes I give up on an eight-hour rest
And give in to the TV's comforting glow instead
With noise
That distracts from the density of the quiet

I'll take the headache of headlines and pings
Over the hallucinogen of the silence
That sends me to the edge of a bad trip

The Poets Will Dream

Even in the fear
The painters will paint
The writers will write
The poets will dream
The musicians will sing
The artists will scream

Creation can be one act of defiant retaliation
A hopeful labor of communal rehabilitation
An inspired catalyst of eye-opening awareness
Or a record for the history books
A meeting point
A joining force

When stomachs knot and churn with the fear of the future
And trigger the fear-wired brain
With hearts pulsing fast
I'm hopeful, if we join our beats
We can harmonize
A melody

So I'll put the pen to the page
As someone else learns to crochet
And a new singer takes to the stage
A comedian makes us laugh in relieving ways
The photographer captures moments of change
While an indie filmmaker opens a portal to a parallel reality
    and an escape

Together, turning the piercing sirens and alarms of fear
Into tunes of hope that have the power to disenchant
    possessed ears

70 Degrees in February in the Northeast

Right now, a lot of the good moments
Feel like a 70-degree day in February on the Northeast coast
It feels kind of wrong
But I'm going to take full advantage of the sun

I'll go for a long walk outside
To feel the warm rays on my shoulders for the first time in months

It shouldn't be this warm in February
The sun a gentle warning—
Among wars, disasters, and political crimes—
The light enjoyment feels wrong during these "*unprecedented times*"
But I've found it best to take advantage of these glimmers while they shine

Shaming myself with guilt hasn't gotten the world very far
Plus, without joy, there's nothing worth fighting for

Texting the Trees

There's a wealth of knowledge on the internet
I can search for virtually anything and find it
But I think I learn more
By talking to the trees—
The trees that have taught me far more about life
Than my thousands of inquiries to ChatGPT

Their knobby trunks have faces that are rooting for me
Carefully watching with wise eyes
As the wind whispers through their leaves and swiftly back to me

On a walk
My phone rests in my pocket
No music or podcast or breaking news—
I prefer to listen to the trees
As they swap secrets
Under the clouds
Revealing their magic
And guiding me to the root
Of self

The trees never deceive me like an online identity
They don't feed me with an algorithm automated to keep me
They don't sell me ideals of beauty
They don't overstimulate me with political propaganda and media
illiteracy

And out of natural curiosity
I plugged famous poems into ChatGPT
And asked for a grade
Just to see
And the computer gave THE Emily Dickinson a C

You see—
The trees grow my creativity
The lichens on their intricate bark recognize artistry

Their rings of age hold memory
Of all the times I've walked by
With tears welling up in my eyes
Because of some guy
Or a job that didn't treat me right
Or the overwhelming pressures of life

Seasonally dropping and reviving their needles or leaves
They're seasoned to understand
Grief
Loss
And empathy

Those feelings that don't always follow fact
And although the internet offers an encyclopedia
Of inspiration and knowledge at my fingertips
This kind of information doesn't capture
The lessons the trees have taught

To explore and address the depth of shadows
In the forest of myself
But to also feel the cheerful sun
Through the tangled branches and their cast shadows
Illuminating me
With my own duality

The lumbering limbs reach to me
To plant the seed of learning
That can't quite be replicated
By technology

Anyway—
The grid might fall apart
And even in the dark
The evergreen trees
Still stand with my heart

The Trees Texted Back

I never had fancy wings
But I remember flying as a kid
Soaring up the steps
Hovering above the driveway

I know I flew
It's not a tampered memory

But as I grew
Gravity got heavy
Year by year
My feet planted
Firmer and firmer
In material reality

Tethered to the dirt
That turned to thick mud
That I could either commit to trudge
By carving my own precarious path
Or by following one of a few tracks
Of the safer cookie-cutter footsteps

I used to fly until I got stuck
Stuck in the mud, caught in the trees
The trees that were once a vibrant green
Until they lost their leaves
Commencing the countdown to Halloween
But since I lost my flight
It's August, then it's Christmas Eve
And every day is another morning
I wake up *not* as the person I want to be

When I could fly, all dreams were in reach
Now, a fairy-dwelling in the woods
Is just sticks, twigs, and moss

Cursed by adult sensibilities
That keep my feet stuck in the mud
Sunken deeper by gravity's pushy fog

That sometimes clears to a window
For adults with open minds
To recalibrate the meaning of magic
That I wished to be pixie dust and wands

The secret I've found
Is that the whimsical wonders
Are hidden within the magnificent monotony
And flightless futility
Of the everyday runaround

So every day *is* another morning
But I wake up no longer searching for a different me
I live to be
And of late, I've noticed
The trees have been glowing a more vibrant green

A Final Farewell, The End, Goodbye?

I've never been good at endings
Clean-cut goodbyes
I specialize in the Once Upon a Time
Strong starts, meaningful middles
That guide me to confront a falling riddle

Exes become friends then exes again
A pattern that lingers until it ends
Trailing off without exact words said
Like quitting jobs
On an impulsive whim
And walking away from conversations
With an awkward dangling sentence

Overthinking my last interaction
The final poem
The closing lines
The concluding word

So, in true fashion
The story is over
With the ending poem in the book

Left unpolished . . .

Unfinished . . .

An imperfect close that opens back up . . .

Acknowledgments

Thank you to my family, for their flexibility to shift with me and their impressive ability to find the humor that always grounds me. My pen would have never been inspired to scribble such coherent sentences if not placed on the page by my well-read mom's hands. Mom, while I've snapped back at your meticulous grammar corrections, I have to admit they've done me good. *Or is it "well"?*

For the dreamer in me, I thank my dad. Dad, the ease with which you turn your ideas into realities has instilled me with the belief that I can do anything. Even if it's delusional, it's gotten me so far as to express appreciation in the permanent pages of my first book.

For my rebellious questioning, my older brother is to blame. Bryan, all those memories of us as kids blasting your alternative and punk music in your room, that grew into teenage humor and adult discussions, molded me more than you know. I'm lucky to have grown up with a friend like you.

For crying and laughing with me when things fall apart, then lifting me up, putting me back together, and expanding my walls, my best friends are the glue. You know who you are! I wouldn't be as tall as I am without your helpful hands, as we lay the bricks and challenge each other to overcome lessons and soar to the highest heights.

For laying a foundation of belief that has expanded my work's reach, I have my internet community to thank. Growing with you, interacting with you, and hearing how my words have impacted your lives has opened my own eyes. You've played a central role in inspiring me to keep my creative spark burning bright.

Finally, I could go on to thank all who have done me wrong, those mean strangers, online haters, and sour endings, but there are also the kind strangers and unexpected silent supporters. The roads I've run a million times, the cities that have held me, my dog who has been beside me through moves and breakups and makeups and more moves, my idols, my enemies. *Everybody* who has played a hand in redirecting me onto this path and strengthening my belief in myself: I wouldn't be writing this if it weren't for you.

Thank you.

Photo by Shortform Media

About the Author

HEIDI BECKER is a writer best known for her signature high-speed internet monologues and viral spoken-word pieces. Blending humor and societal critique with reflective and emotional confessions, Heidi explores the hypnotic chaos of the modern world while bringing her audience on a quest for hope.